PROPHETIC

PRAYER

DECLARATIONS

PROPHETIC PRAYER DECLARATIONS

10 Biblical Affirmations for Spiritual Growth, Birthing, and Breakthroughs

KEMI AKINTEWE, Ph.D.

Institute for New Victory, LLC

Orlando, Florida

Copyright © 2025 by Kemi Akintewe

All rights reserved. This Book or any portion thereof may not be reproduced or used in any manner whatsoever without the express written permission of the publisher except for the use of brief quotations in a book review.

Published and distributed in the United States by the

Institute for New Victory, LLC.

1317 Edgewater Drive, Suite 5364

Orlando, FL 32804

Print ISBN: 979-8-9874126-5-7

e-Book ISBN: 979-8-9874126-6-4

First Edition, March 2025 Printed in the United States of America.

Images by Microsoft©

The author of this Book does not dispense medical advice or prescribe the use of any technique as a form of treatment for physical, emotional, or medical problems without the advice of a physician, either directly or indirectly. The intent of the author is only to offer information of a general nature to help you in your quest for emotional and spiritual well-being. In the event you use any of the information in this Book for yourself, which is your constitutional right, the author and the publisher assume no responsibility for your actions.

All Scripture quotations, unless otherwise indicated, are taken from the Holy Bible, New International Version®, NIV®. Copyright ©1973, 1978, 1984, 2011 by Biblica, Inc.™ Used by permission of Zondervan. All rights reserved worldwide.

Scripture quotations marked AMP are taken from the Amplified® Bible (AMP), copyright © 2015 by The Lockman Foundation. Used by permission. www.lockman.org.

Scripture quotations marked ESV are from the ESV® Bible (The Holy Bible, English Standard Version®), copyright © 2001 by Crossway Bibles, a publishing ministry of Good News Publishers. Used by permission. All rights reserved.

Scripture quotations marked KJV are taken from the King James Version Bible.

Scripture quotations marked NKJV are taken from the New King James Version of the Bible. Copyright © 1982 by Thomas Nelson, Inc. Used by permission. All rights reserved.

Scripture quotations marked NASB are taken from the New American Standard Bible(R), Copyright (C) 1960,1962,1963,1968,1971,1972,1973,1975,1977,1995 by

The Lockman Foundation. Used by permission.

Scripture quotations marked NLT are taken from the Holy Bible, New Living Translation, copyright © 1996, 2004, 2015 by Tyndale House Foundation. All rights reserved. Used by permission.

Scripture quotations marked (WEB) are taken from the World English Bible, public domain.

Scripture quotations marked GNT are from the Good News Translation in Today's English Version- Second Edition Copyright © 1992 by American Bible Society.

Used by Permission.

Scripture quotations marked MSG or "The Message" are taken from The Message. Copyright © 1993, 1994, 1995,

1996, 2000, 2001, 2002. Used by permission of

NavPress Publishing Group.

Scripture quotations marked (CEV) are from the Contemporary English Version Copyright © 1991, 1992, 1995 by American Bible Society. Used by Permission.

Scripture quotations marked "NCV" are taken from the Holy Bible, The New Century Version. Copyright 1987, 1988, 1991. Used by permission of Word Publishing.

Scripture quotations marked ASV are from the American Standard Version of 1901, in the public domain.

Scripture quotations marked CSB have been taken from the Christian Standard Bible®, Copyright © 2017 by Holman Bible Publishers. Used by permission. Christian Standard Bible® and CSB® are federally registered trademarks of Holman Bible Publishers.

Scripture quotations marked (TLB) are taken from The Living Bible, copyright © 1971 by Tyndale House Foundation. Used by permission.

The Holy Bible, Berean Standard Bible, BSB is produced in cooperation with Bible Hub, Discovery Bible, OpenBible.com, and the Berean Bible Translation Committee. This text of God's Word has been dedicated to the public domain.

To my beloved mother, Bernice Ayodeji, who showed me the power of prayers.
I love you!

Table of Contents

INTRODUCTION 9

DECLARATIONS of the 100 NAMES of GOD 28

1. Declarations for Identity and Purpose 34

2. Declarations for Divine Direction and Obedience 41

3. Declarations for Confession, Repentance, and Forgiveness 48

4. Declarations for Consecration and Righteousness 55

5. Declarations for Fruitfulness, Provision, and Increase 63

6. Declarations for Power, Authority, and Dominion 70

7. Declarations for Courage and Overcoming Fear 77

8. Declarations for Victory in Spiritual Warfare 83

9. Declarations for Leadership and Stewardship 89

10. Declarations for Restoration 96

Note to Reader 102

About the Author 103

INTRODUCTION

This *Prophetic Prayer Declarations* book is a collection of powerful scriptures designed to nurture a faith-filled mindset by declaring God's promises over various aspects of your life. I never imagined I could write a book on prayer, since this was an area where I lacked confidence. I felt shy praying in front of others. However, as I matured in my faith, I remember deciding to make improving my prayer life one of my annual goals. God answered my prayers when I joined prayer groups and began interceding for the nation and the needs of others. Different individuals started approaching me for prayers, including non-Christians, and they began sharing the blessings they experienced from our prayers. It became apparent that I would have visions or gain supernatural insights during prayers regarding various situations. Now, I look forward to communicating with God throughout the day, both privately and publicly, without hesitation. I also started studying the different kinds of prayers documented in the Bible, learning how Jesus declared the Word of God to resist Satan's temptation. My daily communion with the Lord led me to write this book.

Introduction

Declarations from scripture have enriched my prayer life and deepened my intimacy with God. When I started declaring His words in prayer, I became bolder, more fearless, and driven by faith. Then, the Lord prompted me to start training others on how to pray. One day, He inspired me to compile my training materials into a book to help the world understand the powerful tool of scripture-based prayers. While I have not yet reached the heights I aspire to in my prayer life, declarative prayers have greatly strengthened my faith, and I hope they benefit you as well. This book serves as a guide for co-creating desirable outcomes through the creative power of the spoken Word of God. Speaking God's Word during prayers allows one to ask intentionally within His will.

Prayers take different forms. A prayer of petition is a fervent and earnest request to fulfill your specific need. An intercessory prayer, or supplication, involves pleading for others, a community, or a nation. Confessional prayer is the acknowledgment of one's sins coupled with seeking forgiveness. Prayers of thanksgiving expresses gratitude and praise for what God has done. Finally, a prayer of affirmations, while less common than the other forms, is the declaration of what is true and right.

Prophetic Prayer Declarations

Declarative prayers are petitions that align with God's prophetic Word. They enable individuals to visualize and believe in their desires and needs as promised by the living Bible. These declarative prayers help us as Christians strengthen our faith and trust in the Almighty God. We can be assured that whatever we ask of Him will be fulfilled if it aligns with His promises. Therefore, declarations are a powerful tool for living out our salvation and fulfilling our God-given purpose.

Declaring your I AM statements sourced from the Word of God enables you to stand firm in your position of victory in Christ, and it is a continuous reminder of your life of freedom in God. The Holy Spirit works within you to guide your path into your identity in Christ and into God's perfect will. Consistently praying with scriptures leads to overcoming life challenges. Any fear, failures, lack, unforgiveness, hate, unrighteousness, fruitlessness, disobedience, and other setbacks have no choice but to flee when one is rooted in God's Word. We have an active weapon to eradicate and overcome the enemy during spiritual warfare.

Prayers cultivate a deeper connection with God. Building a closer relationship with God requires meditating on His Word and obeying its instructions so that you are able to withstand life's daily challenges and combat the

Introduction

pressures of this world. This way of life can reshape your thoughts by changing how you think. Transforming every negative belief into a positive mindset uplifts the individual and brings hope and healing. With this mindset, you can win your battles through God's Word. A reprogramming and spiritual awakening occurs when you are grounded in biblical truths and committed to God's promises.

Prayer is a powerful weapon! The Word of God in Proverbs 18:21 (ESV) states, "Death and life are in the power of the tongue, and those who love it will eat its fruits." When you start making declarations, you are prophesying your reality. Therefore, you have the authority to manifest your realities if you use the potent tool of declarative prayer in your petitions. "For everyone who asks receives" (Matthew 7:8 NLT). A prayer grounded in scripture defines possibilities, unveils God's desire for us—His children—and aligns with His promises. The Bible advises us not to grow weary in prayer (Colossians 4:2). Be intentional in co-creating with the LORD. The Word of God assures us that His word will never return to Him void without accomplishing what it was sent to do (Isaiah 55:11, paraphrased). Don't let your past hinder your requests for today. Do not give up. Wait on the LORD and trust His timing. Declaring His words with faith will yield everlasting fruits. Pray in faith, proclaiming His words always.

> *Don't be weary in prayer; keep at it;*
> *watch for God's answers, and*
> *remember to be thankful when they come*
> *-Colossians 4:2 (TLB)*

There are rules of engagement for declarative prayers. Declaring the Word of God helps shape your outcomes and encourages possibilities. Making prophetic declarations requires an understanding of God's promises. God is committed to what He has said and honors His Word. When your desires align with His promises, you will see results. While patiently waiting, actively engage in experiences that can lead to your desired outcomes. God responds according to His words. Do not become frustrated with unanswered prayers; use scripture to enhance the efficiency of your prayer requests. Fortify your prayers with the Word of God, and always pray for His will.

The declarations in this book consist of twenty-one sets of scriptures tailored for each spiritual area. The first chapter focuses on declarations regarding our **_identity_**, emphasizing who God says we are and His purpose while revealing His plans. Subsequent chapters of

Introduction

scriptural declarations address walking in *divine direction and obedience.* To achieve this consistently, we must embody God's **righteousness** and **consecration** to Him. We must lead a life of continual **confession, repentance, and forgiveness** to grow spiritually. As children of God, part of our rights includes experiencing **fruitfulness, provision,** and **increase.** Moreover, we have the capability to operate with **power, dominion,** and **authority** to combat the enemy's works with *courage, overcome fear*, and gain **victory in spiritual warfare.** Through these declarations, we can truly embrace our **leadership and stewardship** *roles* and experience divine **restoration.**

In summary, scriptural declarations help:

1. Support growth in the knowledge of the Word.
2. Provide a gateway for daily living.
3. Manifest the will of God.
4. Understand and embrace God's promises.
5. Memorize the Word and apply it effectively.
6. Serve as a powerful weapon for spiritual warfare and breakthroughs.
7. Build faith, connection, and trust in God.
8. Facilitate access to the freedom needed to live the life God intended.

9. Replace every lie of the enemy with God's truth, love, and promise.
10. Expand the vision of God's possibilities for one's life.

How to Use This Prayer Guide

Guide for Individual Use

Repentance is encouraged as the first step in seeking Christ's guidance through a declarative scriptural guide. All users must prepare their hearts to receive and be willing to be cleansed of all iniquities. A broken and contrite heart is required for those who wish to receive God's blessings.

To gain significant benefits from this book, it is recommended that you use the declarations for daily prayer. Please refer to the sample prayer provided below. Whenever you encounter a life challenge or feel troubled, you can turn to the chapter that addresses the issue and meditate on the scriptures until they resonate within your spirit. Also, you may

- Begin your day by praying with a chapter of the *Prophetic Prayer Declarations*. You can meditate on one or two of the 21 prayer points in a chapter

Introduction

each day or consider praying with a few scriptures all at once.
- As you declare and decree each point, please launch into your personal request as the Holy Spirit leads.
- Devote at least 15 minutes daily to prayer. Begin with small steps, and as you remain consistent, you will gradually be able to spend more time. While praying, cultivate the habit of pausing to listen to what the LORD says. This may come as a thought, a feeling, or a knowing.
- Capture the declarations you wish to reflect on throughout the day by taking photos, writing them down on your phone, or using Post-it notes for quick access.
- Memorize the word until it becomes part of your vocabulary; It will enter your spirit.
- Before going to bed, pray and meditate on the declarations.

When you consistently pray with these declarations, they become ingrained in you, enabling you to recall them whenever you face opposition or need encouragement. The purpose of these declarations is for you to align with God's word concerning your life. You shape your circumstances and situations, not the other way around. The LORD desires you to prosper in all your endeavors—not in some, but in every aspect of life.

Guide for Group Use

When this prayer book is utilized in communities, churches, or group settings for corporate prayers, the leader can assign some of the 21 prayer points to individuals or lead the prayers alongside them. Once the prayer points are assigned, the leader can trust that the Holy Spirit will work individually from one person to another, resulting in divine encounters and various flows of utterances. Although the book identifies specific areas for prayer, each topic covers multiple aspects of life. Therefore, while praying with the declarations, the leader can mention needs such as the economy, the nation, jobs, faith, marriages, children, health, and careers as directed by the Holy Spirit.

Please allow the Holy Spirit to guide the prayer sessions fully. Prophesy as inspired by the Holy Spirit. Keep a pen and journal nearby to record your thoughts.

In general, always have an attitude of praise, gratitude, and adoration. Command every spirit of distraction, pride, shame, and unforgiveness to leave you in Jesus' name. Approach the LORD humbly with your sins, weaknesses, and vulnerabilities. There is no more

Introduction

shame. You have been redeemed and set free. Ask the LORD for your wants and needs as needed. Be prepared to hear from Him as well. The *Prophetic Prayer Declarations* enable us to prophesy the LORD's promises over our lives and help fill our atmosphere with God's revelations. As you abide in His Word, divine encounters are sure to manifest.

Prophetic Prayer Declarations

Sample Prayer Declarations

The scriptures in the *Prophetic Prayer Declarations* book have been adapted to the I Am format to make them personable. Multiple Bible translations are incorporated throughout this book to accommodate readers of all levels. Certain verses have been paraphrased to enhance relatability. Readers may refer to their preferred versions in sections where a translation is not specified.

Sample prayers are provided below to guide you in how to engage with each scripture. Please do not restrict yourself to just this format. Instead, allow the Holy Spirit to direct you on how to use them. Each declaration should inspire a prayer point in your life. Once you receive inspiration through your thoughts, feelings, or knowledge about something you should pray for, please act on it because it is most likely the prompting from the Holy Spirit.

Introduction

1. Suggestion on how to use the **Declarations for Fruitfulness, Provision, and Increase** Chapter:

I decree that as I ask, I will receive; as I seek, I will find; when I knock, the door will be opened to me. As I ask, the LORD will make the nations my inheritance and the ends of the earth my possession (Matthew 7:7 GNT and Psalm 2:8 NIV).

Dear LORD,

I decree that as I ask, I will receive; as I seek, I will find; when I knock, the door will be opened to me. As I ask, the LORD will make the nations my inheritance and the ends of the earth my possession. Father, I thank You for Your promises. I pray for a financial breakthrough regarding my debts. Provide various opportunities to boost my earning potential. I ask for open doors in my career. LORD, open the doors for promotion and elevation, and grant me acceleration. Please close every door that the enemy has opened in my life. And shut every unfruitful door, the door of malice, lack, strife, and bitterness, in Jesus's name.

Amen.

Prophetic Prayer Declarations

2. Suggestion on how to use the **Declarations for Restoration** Chapter:

I decree the LORD is making all things new. I receive a new heart and a new spirit within me (Revelation 21:5 and Ezekiel 36:26).

Heavenly Father,
I declare that You are making all things new. I receive a new heart and a new spirit within me. LORD, I ask that You restore my divine position. I release myself from the guilt of sin and shame. Deliver me from the spirit of shame, falsehood, and every lie of the enemy. I repent of my past ways and ungodliness. I separate myself from my old reputation. No more pouring old wine into new wineskins. Thank You for Your mercy and grace in my life. For whom the LORD has set free is free indeed. Today, I am free and ready to fulfill my God-given assignment in Jesus's name.
Amen.

Introduction

Author's Prayer for the Readers

Dear LORD,
As the reader engages with these prophetic prayer declarations in this book, I pray they take time to meditate on Your Word. May Your promises be a guiding light in their lives, permeating every aspect of their being. Allow Your Word to inspire transformation in their relationship with You. I ask for an intimate relationship with You, the ability to discern Your Spirit, and for their prayer life to flourish. I pray for divine encounters, open doors, and breakthroughs. Heavenly Father, through these powerful prayers, awaken every dream and vision that has laid dormant in their lives, in Jesus' name.
Amen

And for you, reader,

I pray the Word of God will permeate your heart and mind. I decree you will gain authority over your thoughts. This season, your mind will be a fertile ground for thinking positively and creatively so that you live as co-creators with God to change any undesirable situation toward a desirable outcome.

Prophetic Prayer Declarations

I pray that you will lay hold of a miracle-working power that will lift you from confusion, misery, melancholy, and failure and guide you to your rightful position in Christ. May He resolve your mysteries, sever you from emotional and physical bondage, and set you on the royal road to freedom, happiness, and peace of mind.

As you use this book, I pray you awaken to a new life filled with power and divine opportunities. I pray that the LORD grants you dominion and a great platform to shine for His glory. May the LORD sharpen your gifts. May the anointing that provokes divine favor and brings supernatural encounters be yours in Jesus' name.
Amen

Introduction

Birthing: Get Ready for a New Season, A New You

Positioning is everything! Are you ready to give birth to God's purpose for your life? To bring your purpose to fruition, you must stay connected to Almighty God and keep your focus on what He says about you and the vision He has placed within you. Life often tries to distract us from our divine purpose through work, health challenges, relationships, and finances; however, we must refuse to remain down for too long. "Do not be afraid. Stand firm, and you will see the deliverance the LORD will bring you today. The obstacles [Egyptians] you see today, you will never see again. The LORD will fight for you; you need only to be still" (Exodus 14:13-14). For the Israelites to escape Egypt in Exodus 14:15-28, God instructed Moses to take his position, make a move, raise the staff, and stretch out his hand. God loves you and desires for you to succeed in every area of your life. As you remain close to God, He will provide divine instructions for your new season. A season might stretch you, but it won't break you. You cannot enter a new season unless you show up for the present one.

Would you allow God to take the driver's seat? Would you surrender to Him? You are destined for His glory.

Prophetic Prayer Declarations

Claim every scripture found in this prayer book. Believe it, live it, and continue declaring it until you fully embody what the LORD says about you. God says you are chosen, a royal priesthood, and His special possession (1 Peter 2:9 Paraphrased). With this understanding, you must walk in victory.

In the natural sense, birthing involves a process of preparation, the investment of time, discernment, and forbearance to bring something new to life. Similarly, spiritually, birthing new seasons may require disciplining your soul and spirit to grow and transform into the image and likeness of God. While the past lies behind you, the birth of newness in your life is ahead. Bridging the gap between where you have been and where you need to be might only take a season. David began as just a shepherd, and he was anointed to be a King in one moment. Your current position serves as preparation for your future. God holds the keys to unlock the seasons in your life. Utilize this book to declare His promises over your life. Are you ready to speak to your next season? Start declaring the affirmations that resonate with you the most. These declarations can help counter any lies you believe about God, yourself, and the world we inhabit with His truth, goodness, and beauty.

Introduction

God's Word can change seasons. The Word we speak is Spirit and life. Let the Word of God not depart from your mouth. "For they are life to those who find them, and healing and health to all their flesh" (Proverbs 4:22 AMP).

Now is your divine moment! Make the decision by declaring that:

I am entering a new season with a
spirit-filled mindset,
supernatural manifestations, and divine patterns.
I surrender everything to the LORD Almighty!

Prophetic Prayer Declarations

Date _____

My Desires in this Season

Write down your prayer requests. State what you want the Lord to do for you as you position yourself to receive from Him.

_____

_____

_____

_____

_____

_____

_____

_____

_____

_____

_____

Take delight in the LORD, and he will give you your heart's desires.
-Psalms 37:4 (NLT)

DECLARATIONS
of the 100 NAMES of GOD

In Amos 3:3, the bible says, "Can two walk together unless they agree?" There is power in unity when individuals agree and align with one another. How much more when we walk together in agreement with God? It is crucial that you are in partnership with God as you navigate the ups and downs of life together. When you do, Psalms 16:11 says the LORD will reveal your path of life, filling you with joy in His presence and providing eternal pleasures.

Always seek God's presence and stay focused on Him. Pray with awareness of His presence while avoiding distractions from your surroundings. Do not dwell on your problems. Instead, concentrate on the problem solver. When we are in God's presence, we are spiritually fortified, our intimacy deepens, we learn to understand His ways more clearly, and we gain wisdom and guidance for our everyday lives.

While praying, be still before the LORD and patiently wait for Him to speak (Psalm 37:7). Be conscious and envision that God is near you. Be mindful of who you are

Prophetic Prayer Declarations

praying to, His character, and His glorious nature, praise Him, and call on His following names:

1. Our Father (Abba)
2. Eternal God (El Olam)
3. Healer (Jehovah Rapha)
4. Peace (Jehovah Shalom)
5. Righteousness (Jehovah Tsidkenu)
6. Ever Present (Jehovah Shammah)
7. My Shepherd (Jehovah Raah)
8. My Banner (Jehovah Nissi)
9. My Sanctifier (Jehovah Kadesh)
10. My Provider (Jehovah Jireh)
11. My Maker (Hoseenu)
12. My Rock (Tsuri)
13. My Helper (Azar)
14. My Redeemer
15. My Pillar
16. My Fortress
17. My Refuge
18. Creator (Elohim)
19. The LORD Most High (El Elyon)
20. The LORD of Hosts (Jehovah Sabaoth)
21. The God Who Sees Me (Jehovah El Roi)
22. The Great High Priest
23. The Light of the world

DECLARATIONS Of The 100 NAMES Of GOD

24. The Life, the Truth, and the Way
25. The Same Yesterday, Today, and Forever
26. The Beginning and the End (Alpha and Omega)
27. The Bright and Morning Star
28. The Gate
29. The Word
30. The Rock of Ages
31. The Lamb of God
32. The Resurrection and the Life
33. The Chief Cornerstone
34. The Salt of the Earth
35. The Living Stone
36. The Author and Finisher of Our Faith
37. The Fountain of Living Water
38. The Lion of the Tribe of Judah
39. The Heir of All Things
40. The Faithful and True Witness
41. Horn of Salvation
42. Immanuel, God is with us
43. King of Kings
44. Prince of Peace
45. Author of Life
46. My Strong Tower
47. Consuming Fire
48. Way Maker
49. Messiah

Prophetic Prayer Declarations

50. Shiloh
51. Friend
52. Watchman
53. Wonderful Counselor
54. Master
55. Bridegroom
56. Captain
57. Ruler
58. Seer
59. Intercessor
60. Prophet
61. Teacher
62. Evangelist
63. Apostle
64. Avenger
65. Protector
66. Deliverer
67. Defender
68. Rebuilder
69. Restorer
70. Refiner
71. Purifier
72. Potter
73. Transformer
74. Justifier
75. Supplier

DECLARATIONS Of The 100 NAMES Of GOD

76. Mediator
77. Baptizer
78. Advocate
79. Savior
80. Branch
81. Righteous Judge
82. Victorious One
83. Faithful One
84. Gracious One
85. Glorious Hope
86. Holy One
87. Holy Spirit
88. Ancient of Days
89. Great, I Am
90. Bread from Heaven
91. Bread of Life
92. Miracle Worker
93. True Vine
94. Dayspring
95. Omnipotent
96. Omnipresence
97. Omniscient
98. Jesus Christ (Yeshua)
99. The LORD (Adonai)
100. God Almighty (El Shaddai)

Prophetic Prayer Declarations

Date _____

Reflection

Choose a few names of God from the list. Reflect on why those names are significant to you in this season of your life. Then, write down your thoughts.

_____
_____
_____
_____
_____
_____
_____
_____
_____
_____
_____
_____

Call to Me, and I will answer you, and show you great and mighty things, which you do not know
-Jeremiah 33:3 (NKJV)

Chapter 1
Declarations for Identity and Purpose

Knowing our identity in Christ allows us to walk in purpose. The Apostle Paul was a prosecutor of Christians before he encountered Jesus Christ on his way to persecute believers, and then he took on a new identity as an apostle of Christ. Paul is known to have written at least one-third of the New Testament. The statements below speak to the identity you have in Christ. Ask the LORD to reveal, confirm, or validate your identity and purpose.

1. I am a new creation in Christ. I decree old things have passed away; all things have become new (2 Corinthians 5:17 NKJV).
2. I share in the inheritance of God's holy people in the kingdom of light (Colossians 1:12b).
3. I am a chosen generation, a royal priesthood, a holy nation, a peculiar person. I declare I will

show forth the praises of God who has called me out of darkness into his marvelous light (1 Peter 2: 9 KJV).

4. I am God's workmanship, created in Christ Jesus for good works (Ephesians 2:10a ESV).
5. I have been crucified with Christ. It is no longer I who live, but Christ who lives in me. And the life I now live in the flesh, I live by faith in the Son of God, who loved me and gave himself for me (Galatians 2:20).
6. I am raised with Christ and seated with you, LORD, in the heavenly realms because I am united with Christ Jesus (Ephesians 2:6 NLT).
7. I live my life in God, rooted and built up in him, strengthened in the faith overflowing with thankfulness. I walk in union with Christ, reflecting His character in the things I do and say. I live a life that leads others away from sin (Colossians 2:6-7 NIV, AMP).
8. I have the love of Christ, which far surpasses knowledge. I am filled up with all the fullness of God. I have the richest experience of God's presence in my life, completely filled and flooded with God Himself (Ephesians 3:18 AMP).
9. I decree that the eyes of my heart are enlightened in order that I may know the hope to which God

Declarations for Identity and Purpose

has called me, the riches of his glorious inheritance in His holy people (Ephesians 1:18 NIV).

10. I and the children whom the LORD has given me! We are for signs and wonders (Isaiah 8:18).
11. I am a child of God, and I have overcome the world because greater is He that is in me than He that is in the world (I John 4: 4 KJV).
12. I have the Spirit of Jesus, who was raised from the dead living inside me. His mighty power is far above any ruler, authority, power, leader, or anything else (Romans 8:11 NIV and Ephesians 1:19-21 NLT).
13. I declare that nothing shall separate me from the love of Christ. No trouble or hardship or persecution or famine or nakedness or danger or sword. I am more than a conqueror through Christ, who loved me. I am convinced that neither death nor life, neither angels nor demons, neither the present nor the future, nor any powers, neither height nor depth nor anything else in all creation, will be able to separate me from the love of God that is in Christ Jesus our LORD (Romans 8: 35, 37-39 NIV).
14. I know that in all things, God works for my good, and I am called according to His purpose. Since

Prophetic Prayer Declarations

God is for me, no one can be against me (Romans 8:28 NIV).

15. I decree, never again shall I be called the forsaken or the one that God forgot. My new name will be "The One God's Delight and "The Bride," for the LORD delights in me and will claim me as his own. God will rejoice over me as a bridegroom with his bride (Isaiah 62:4-5 TLB).

16. I am set apart. Before I was formed in my mother's womb, God knew me. Before I was born, He set me apart; He appointed me to the nations (Jeremiah 1:5). The Spirit of the LORD is on me because He has anointed me to proclaim good news to the poor and to heal the brokenhearted (Luke 4:18 NIV, TLB).

17. I give thanks to God because I am awesomely and wonderfully made. Wonderful are God's works, and my soul knows it very well. My frame was not hidden from God when He made me in secret and skillfully formed me in the depths of the earth. He saw me before I was born and scheduled each day of my life before I began to breathe. Every day was recorded in His book! (Psalm 139:13-15 NASB and Psalm 139:16 TLB).

Declarations for Identity and Purpose

18. I know the plans the LORD has for me. They are plans for good and not for evil, to give me a future and hope (Jeremiah 29:11).
19. I can make many plans, but the LORD's purpose will prevail (Proverbs 19:21).
20. Whatever I do, I do it all to the glory of God. I do not become a stumbling block to others. I seek the good of many, that they may be saved (1 Corinthians 10:31-33 BSB).
21. I have been given all authority in heaven and on earth to go and make disciples of all the nations, baptizing them in the name of the Father and the Son and the Holy Spirit. And to teach these new disciples to obey all the commands Jesus has given me (Matthew 28:18-20 NLT).

Prophetic Prayer Declarations

Date _____

Reflection

1. How is your identity revealed through the knowledge of the Word of God? Write down your revelations.

_____

_____

_____

_____

_____

_____

_____

_____

_____

_____

_____

God's Spirit touches our spirits and confirms who we really are. We know who he is, and we know who we are: Father and children.
-Romans 8:16 (MSG)

Declarations for Identity and Purpose

2. Seek the Lord in prayers for your divine purpose guided by declarations 4 & 9. Write down your revelations.

_____

_____

_____

_____

_____

_____

_____

_____

_____

_____

_____

_____

_____

For still, the vision awaits its appointed time; it hastens to the end—it will not lie. If it seems slow, wait for it; it will surely come; it will not delay.
-Habakkuk 2:3 (ESV)

Chapter 2
Declarations for Divine Direction and Obedience

When we obey God's words, He is committed to ordering our steps and providing divine direction. For the Israelites to leave Egypt and walk away from captivity, their leader Moses followed all of God's instructions on how to deal with the King of Egypt. Then the LORD successfully led them to their promised land. What is it that you are seeking guidance on? Ask the LORD for divine direction and the grace to obey His instructions as you study these declarations.

1. I declare this is the day the LORD has made. I shall rejoice and be glad in it. I declare my path is straight and smooth. All obstacles that want to block my way are removed (Psalm 118:24 and Proverbs 3: 5-6 AMP).

Declarations for Divine Direction and Obedience

2. God is within me; I shall not be moved. LORD, help me through every new day (Psalm 46:5).
3. I am taught by the LORD what He wants me to do. I am led by the LORD along a safe path (Psalm 27:11 GNT).
4. I decree that my path is like the dawning light that shines more and more until the perfect day (Proverbs 4:18 WEB).
5. I declare that God will give me every place where I set my foot. Wherever I go and whatever I do, I will be blessed (Joshua 1:3 NIV and Deuteronomy 28:6 NLT).
6. I am always led by the LORD. You, LORD, satisfy me in a parched land and strengthen my bones. I am like a watered garden and like a spring whose water never runs dry (Isaiah 58:11 CSB).
7. I have a beautiful inheritance. The lines have fallen for me in pleasant places. I set the LORD always before me. Because the LORD is at my right hand. I will not be shaken (Psalm 16:6, 8 ESV).
8. I demolish arguments and every pretension that sets itself up against the knowledge of God, and I take captive every thought to make it obedient to Christ (2 Corinthians 10:5 NIV).

Prophetic Prayer Declarations

9. God's Word is a lamp to my feet and a light to my path (Psalm 119:105 NKJV).
10. LORD, you know my ways, and you pay attention to them. When I am tested, I will come forth as refined gold, pure and luminous (Job 23:10 AMP).
11. I declare that my steps are ordered by the LORD. LORD, I know you care about every detail of my life. You have given me another helper: a Comforter, Advocate, Intercessor, Counselor, Strengthener, and the Holy Spirit is with me forever. He will teach me all things. And He will help me remember everything Christ said. (Psalm 37:23 NLT and John 14:26 AMP).
12. When I walk, my steps will not be hampered; when I run, I will not stumble. I will not set my foot on the path of the wicked or walk in the way of evildoers (Proverb 4:12, 14 NIV).
13. I am an obedient child of God, and I do not conform to evil desires. (1 Peter 1:14).
14. I do not merely listen to the Word of God. I do what it says (James 1:22 NIV).
15. I love the LORD my God, and I will keep his requirements, his decrees, his laws, and his commands always (Deuteronomy 11:1).

Declarations for Divine Direction and Obedience

16. As I ask, LORD, tell me remarkable secrets that I do not know about things to come (Jeremiah 33:3)
17. My steps are established by the LORD. I go from strength to strength (Proverbs 16:9 and Psalms 84:7).
18. I am God's treasured possession. LORD, protect me from all danger and keep me safe. LORD, protect me as I come and go, now and forever (Exodus 19:5 NIV and Psalm 121: 7-8 GNT).
19. I am a wise person who built my house on the rock. Even if the rain falls and the floods come, and the winds blow and beat on the house, it won't fall because my house is founded on the rock (Matthew 7:24-26).
20. I declare the LORD's blessing is upon me. I will surely multiply as the stars of heaven and the sand on the seashore. And my offspring shall possess the gate of my enemies, and in my offspring shall all the nations of the earth be blessed (Genesis 22:17-18).
21. I am strong and very courageous. The Word of God shall not depart from my mouth. I shall meditate on it day and night. I will carefully obey the Word of God. I will not turn from it to the right or the left. I declare that my way is prosperous

Prophetic Prayer Declarations

and will be successful wherever I go (Joshua 1:7-8 NLT).

Declarations for Divine Direction and Obedience

Date _____

Reflection

1. How is the LORD ordering your steps during this season of your life? In what direction are you being led? Write down your revelations.

_____
_____
_____
_____
_____
_____
_____
_____
_____
_____
_____

Order my steps in thy word; and let not any iniquity have dominion over me.
-Psalm 119:133 (KJV)

Prophetic Prayer Declarations

2. Seek the Lord in prayers to reveal any obstacles hindering you from fulfilling declarations 13 - 15. Write down your revelations.

_____

_____

_____

_____

_____

_____

_____

_____

_____

_____

_____

_____

_____

_____

Seek his will in all you do, and he will show you which path to take.
-Proverbs 3:6 (NLT)

Chapter 3
Declarations for Confession, Repentance, and Forgiveness

A prayer of confession involves acknowledging wrongdoings and seeking forgiveness. After King David sinned, he felt remorse for his actions. He confessed, repented, and asked for forgiveness. Repentance means being convicted of sin, committing to change, turning away from sin and drawing closer to God. We cannot continue in sin and expect grace to increase (Romans 6:1). Christ died for our sins and will forgive them if we confess. Ask the LORD to reveal any hidden sins as you study these declarations.

1. LORD, I seek your face; forgive me of my sins and heal me. I decree that as I confess my sins to others and pray for others, I will be healed (2 Chronicles 7:14 ESV and James 5:16 NIV).

Prophetic Prayer Declarations

2. I do not let sin control the way I live. I do not give in to sinful desires. I do not allow any part of my body to become an instrument of evil to serve sin. Instead, I give myself completely to God. I use my whole body as an instrument to do what is right for the glory of God (Romans 6: 11-13 NLT).
3. I repent and turn from my sins. I don't let sin destroy me! I put all my rebellion behind me. I don't repay evil for evil. I don't retaliate with insults when people insult me. Instead, I pay them back with a blessing (Ezekiel 18:30–31 NLT and 1 Peter 3:9 NLT).
4. I praise the LORD, my soul, and forget not all his benefits. The LORD forgives all my sins and heals all my diseases. He redeems my life from the pit and crowns me with love and compassion. He satisfies my desires with good things so that my youth is renewed like the eagle's (Psalm 103:2-5 NIV).
5. As far as the East is from the West, so far has God removed my transgressions from me. I am set free in Christ Jesus from the law of sin and death (Psalm 103:12 NKJV and Romans 8:2 ESV).

Declarations for Confession, Repentance, and Forgiveness

6. I decree that I am set free from sin, and I have become a slave to righteousness (Romans 6:18 NIV).
7. I declare that as I confess my sins, the LORD is faithful and just and will forgive my sins and purify me from all unrighteousness (1 John 1:9 NIV). Cleanse me, and I will be clean. Wash me, and I will be whiter than snow (Psalm 51:7 NIV).
8. I decree I am free from all bitterness, rage, anger, brawling, and slander, along with every form of malice (Ephesians 4:31 NIV).
9. I am kind, tender-hearted, and forgive others, as God has forgiven me through Christ (Ephesians 4:32 GNT).
10. I will make allowance for others' faults and forgive anyone who offends me (Colossians 3:13 NLT).
11. I will forget what is behind me and do my best to reach what is ahead. I press toward the mark for the prize of the high calling of God in Christ Jesus (Philippians 3:13 GNT, 14 KJV).
12. I do not take revenge on others or continue to hate them, but I love my neighbor as myself (Leviticus 19:18 GNT).
13. LORD, blot out all my iniquity. Create in me a pure heart, O God, and renew a steadfast spirit within me. Do not cast me from your presence or

take your Holy Spirit from me (Psalm 51:9-10 NIV).

14. I have hidden the Word of God in my heart so that I might not sin against him. I carry God's incorruptible seed inside of me; I will not go on sinning because I have been born of God (Psalm 119:11 and 1 John 3:9 NIV).
15. Sin is no longer my master, for I no longer live under the requirements of the law. Instead, I live under the freedom of God's grace (Romans 6: 14 NLT).
16. I am not easily angered. I keep no records of wrongs. I am slow to anger, and I have the power to overlook offenses (1 Corinthians 13:4-6 NIV and Proverbs 19:11).
17. I do not let my anger cause me shame, nor allow it to last until the sun goes down (Ephesians 4:26 AMP).
18. I am getting rid of everything that slows me down, especially the sin that just won't let go. And I am determined to run the race that is ahead of me (Hebrews 12:1 CEV).
19. I clothe myself with compassion, kindness, humility, gentleness, and patience. (Colossians 3:12 NIV).

Declarations for Confession, Repentance, and Forgiveness

20. I press on to take hold of that for which Christ Jesus took hold of me. I do not consider myself yet to have taken hold of it. But one thing I do is forgetting what is behind and straining toward what is ahead. I press on toward the goal to win the prize for which God has called me heavenward in Christ Jesus (Philippians 3:12-14).

21. I forgive my brothers and sisters who sin against me seventy-seven times. I forgive others as the LORD has forgiven me (Matthew 18:21–22; 6:12).

Prophetic Prayer Declarations

Date _____

Reflection

1. Are you seeking healing in your life? What comes to mind as you reflect on declarations 1 & 4? Write down your revelations.

_____

_____

_____

_____

_____

_____

_____

_____

_____

_____

_____

Therefore confess your sins to each other and pray for each other so that you may be healed. The prayer of a righteous person is powerful and effective.
-James 5:16 (NIV)

Declarations for Confession, Repentance, and Forgiveness

2. What offences should I make allowance for in declarations 10 – 12? Write down your revelations.

_____
_____
_____
_____
_____
_____
_____
_____
_____
_____
_____
_____
_____
_____
_____

If possible, as far as it depends on you, live at peace with everyone.
-Romans 12:18 (AMP)

Chapter 4
Declarations for Consecration and Righteousness

Righteousness and consecration are interdependent virtues for believers. Consecration involves being separated from sin, uncleanness, or anything disapproved by God, in order to live a life fully devoted to His will. Righteousness is the practice of living faithfully and justly according to the Word of God. Jesus exemplified a consecrated and righteous life. He was humble, spiritual, pure, and dedicated to the things of God. Are you prepared to live a righteous and consecrated life? Ask the LORD for strength, will, and power for righteous living and consecration as you study these declarations.

1. I declare that I am filled with the fruit of righteousness, which comes through Jesus

Declarations for Consecration and Righteousness

Christ, to the glory and praise of God (Philippians 1:11 NIV).

2. I put to death sexual immorality, impurity, lust, evil desires, and greed; anger, rage, malice, slander, and filthy language (Colossians 3:5). Rather, I am clothed with compassion, kindness, humility, gentleness, and patience (Colossians 3:12b).
3. I deny myself and take up the cross daily and follow Christ (Luke 9:23, NASB).
4. I throw off my old sinful nature and my former way of life, which was corrupted by lust and deception. I let the Spirit of God renew my thoughts and attitude. I put on my new self, created to be like God in true righteousness and holiness (Ephesians 4:22-23 NLT, 24 NIV).
5. I do not let any unwholesome talk come out of my mouth, but only what helps build others up according to their needs, that it may benefit those who listen (Ephesians 4:29 NIV).
6. I claim my love for Christ has become increasingly rich with knowledge and all kinds of insight. I decree that I will be able to decide what really matters and be sincere and blameless (Philippians 1:9-10 CEB).

Prophetic Prayer Declarations

7. I stand firm in all the will of God, mature and fully assured. I have nothing to do with the fruitless deeds of darkness (Colossians 4:12 and Ephesians 5:11 NIV).
8. I declare I am filled with the Spirit of the Almighty God. I speak to others with psalms, hymns, and songs from the Spirit (Ephesians 5:18-19 NIV). I am quick to hear, slow to speak, and slow to anger (James 1:19 ESV).
9. I pay attention to God's Word. I do not lose sight of them; I keep them within my heart. For they are life to those who find them and health to my whole body. I guard my heart with all diligence, for from it flow springs of life. I put away deception from my mouth; I keep my lips from perverse speech. I fix my gaze straight ahead and make a level path for my feet. I do not swerve to the right or to the left. I turn my feet away from evil (Proverbs 4: 20-27 BSB).
10. I meditate on the Word of God day and night, so I carefully obey everything written in it. I decree that I will prosper and succeed in all I do (Joshua 1:8 NLT).
11. The LORD is my hiding place and my shield. I wait for the Word of God to guide me. The Scripture teaches, rebukes, corrects, and trains

me in righteousness, so I am thoroughly equipped for every good work. (Psalms 119: 114 AMP and 2 Timothy 3:16-17 NIV).

12. I firmly hold to the Word of Life. I declare that I live a clean and innocent life as a child of God. I shine like bright lights in this world, and I will not run my race in vain. My work will be useful (Philippians 2:15-16 NLT).
13. I decree I have the Spirit of power, love, and self-control (2 Timothy 1:6-7 GNT).
14. I declare that I think continually on whatever is true, whatever is honorable and worthy of respect, whatever is right and confirmed by God's Word, whatever is pure and wholesome, whatever is lovely and brings peace, whatever is admirable and of good repute; if there is any excellence, if there is anything worthy of praise center my mind on them and implant them in my heart (Philippians 4:8 AMP).
15. I do not associate with anyone who claims to be a brother or sister but is sexually immoral or greedy, an idolater or slanderer, a drunkard or swindler (1 Corinthians 5:11 NIV).
16. I am ruled by the peace of Christ in my heart (Colossians 3:15). I have a gentle spirit. I am gracious, unselfish, merciful, tolerant, and

patient, which is known to all people (Philippians 4:5 AMP).

17. I am an ambassador for Christ and reconciled to God. God made Christ, who knew no sin, to be sin on my behalf so that I might become the righteousness of God in Him (2 Corinthians 5:20-21 NASB). I am becoming the righteousness of God.

18. I receive the Spirit of wisdom and revelation so that I know Christ better. I also receive a greater understanding in my heart, so I'll know the hope to which Christ has called me and that I know how rich and glorious the blessings God has promised his holy people (Ephesians 1:17, NCV).

19. LORD, rescue me from the evil one. I do not yield to temptation; instead, I overcome it with the Word of God. God is faithful. The LORD will not allow the temptation to be more than I can stand. When I'm tempted, He will show me a way out so that I can endure. (Matthew 6:13 NLT and 1 Corinthians 10:13).

20. I come out of darkness, and I am separated. I am not unequally yoked with unbelievers. I am the temple of the living God. God dwells with me and walks with me. I touch no unclean thing (2 Corinthians 6: 14,16-17 BSB).

Declarations for Consecration and Righteousness

21. I live a life worthy of the LORD and please him in every way: bearing fruit in every good work, growing in the knowledge of God (Colossians 1:10 NIV).

Prophetic Prayer Declarations

Date _____

Reflection

1. From declarations 19, what do you want to be rescued from? Are there temptations that are a thorn in your flesh? Write down your revelations.

_____

_____

_____

_____

_____

_____

_____

_____

_____

_____

_____

So I say, let the Holy Spirit guide your lives. Then you won't be doing what your sinful nature craves..
-Galatians 5:16 (NLT)

Declarations for Consecration and Righteousness

2. How would you live a consecrated and righteous life? What scriptures do you need to help support your strategy? Write down your revelations.

_____

_____

_____

_____

_____

_____

_____

_____

_____

_____

_____

_____

_____

_____

_____

_____

I seek you with all my heart; do not let me stray from your commands.
-Psalm 119:10 (NIV)

Chapter 5
Declarations for Fruitfulness, Provision, and Increase

Part of God's promises for those who obey is that they will be lenders, not borrowers (Deuteronomy 15: 6). Jacob experienced God's blessings of fruitfulness, provision, and increase. God blessed him with children, food, and wealth, and even birthed the whole nation of Israel through him. Is there something you have been seeking? Ask the LORD for His supernatural blessings as you reflect on these declarations.

1. I seek first the kingdom of God and His righteousness. I am not worried about missing out. My Heavenly Father knows my needs and will meet them all (Matthew 6: 33-34).
2. I flourish like a palm tree. I will grow like a cedar of Lebanon, planted in the house of the LORD. I will flourish in the courts of our God. I will still bear

Declarations for Fruitfulness, Provision, and Increase

fruit in old age, staying fresh and green, proclaiming, "The LORD is upright; he is my Rock, and there is no wickedness in him."(Psalms 92: 12-15 NIV).

3. I am fruitful. I multiply and fill the earth and subdue it. I have dominion over the fish of the sea and over the birds of the heavens and over every living thing that moves on the earth (Genesis 1:28 KJV).

4. I command any darkness around me to turn to the brightness of noon. The LORD will always guide me and satisfy me with good things. He will keep me strong and well. I will be like a garden that has plenty of water, like a spring of water that never goes dry (Isaiah 58: 10-11 GNT).

5. I am not anxious about anything. But in every situation, by prayer and petition, with thanksgiving, I present my request to you, LORD (Philippians 4:6-7 NIV).

6. I believe in the almighty God. I declare that rivers of living water will flow from within me (John 7:38 NIV).

7. I worship the LORD, my God. He will bless me with food and water and take away my sicknesses. I will not miscarry or be barren. He will give me a long life (Exodus 23:25-25 GNT).

Prophetic Prayer Declarations

8. I am loaded daily with benefits from God. He is my salvation (Psalm 68:19). The LORD shall supply all my needs according to his riches in glory by Christ Jesus (Philippians 4:19 KJV).
9. God will generously provide for all my needs. I will always have everything I need and plenty left over to share with others (2 Corinthians 9:8 NLT).
10. As I give, I will receive. My gift will return to me in full, pressed down, shaken together to make room for more, running over, and poured into my lap. The amount I give will determine the amount I get back (Luke 6:38 NLT).
11. I speak God's Word; it will always produce fruit. It will accomplish all I want it to, and it will prosper everywhere I send it (Isaiah 55:11 NLT).
12. I declare that my gift finds expression, and I am a blessing to others (Luke 4:18).
13. I am blessed and protected by the LORD. He smiles on me and is gracious to me. The LORD showers me with divine favors and gives me peace (Numbers 6: 24-26).
14. I seek the LORD, so I lack no good thing (Psalms 34:10 ESV). I have everything I need because the LORD is my Shepherd (Psalms 23:1 TLB).
15. I take delight in the LORD, and He will give me the desires of my heart (Psalm 37: 4 NIV).

Declarations for Fruitfulness, Provision, and Increase

16. I declare the LORD shall perfect everything that concerns me (Psalm 138:8). He will grant me abundant prosperity. He will send rain in season and bless all my work so that I will lend to many nations, but I will not have to borrow from any (Deuteronomy 28:11-12).

17. I decree that as I ask, I will receive; as I seek, I will find; when I knock, the door will be opened to me. As I ask, the LORD will make the nations my inheritance and the ends of the earth my possession (Matthew 7:7 GNT and Psalm 2:8 NIV).

18. I decree that God, who is able, through his mighty power at work within me, will accomplish infinitely more than I might ask or think (Ephesians 3:20 NLT).

19. God will greatly bless me and enlarge my territory. LORD, be with me and keep me from anything evil that might cause me pain (1 Chronicles 4:10).

20. I claim God's promise. He will surely treat me kindly and will multiply my descendants until they become as numerous as the sands along the seashore—too many to count (Genesis 32:12 NLT).

Prophetic Prayer Declarations

21. I am like a tree planted by streams of water, which which yields its fruit in season and whose leaf does not wither; whatever I do prospers (Psalms 1:3 NIV).

Declarations for Fruitfulness, Provision, and Increase

Date _____

Reflection

1. What are your needs? Where are you seeking an increase? Write down your revelations.

_____

_____

_____

_____

_____

_____

_____

_____

_____

_____

_____

_____

The lions may grow weak and hungry, but those who seek the Lord lack no good thing.
-Psalm 34:10 (NIV)

Prophetic Prayer Declarations

2. What actions can you take as you wait on the Lord for His provision? Review declarations 5, 7, 14, 15, and 21. Write down your revelations.

_____
_____
_____
_____
_____
_____
_____
_____
_____
_____
_____
_____
_____

Yes, I am the vine; you are the branches. Those who remain in me, and I in them, will produce much fruit. For apart from me you can do nothing.
-John 15:5 (NLT)

Chapter 6
Declarations for Power, Authority, and Dominion

Power, authority, and dominion define our capacity to rule over issues in and around our lives. Jesus overcame Satan's tactics by exercising His rights. Christ has all authority and power in heaven and on earth. Believers have this immeasurable greatness of His power (Ephesians 1:19). Are you exercising your divine power, authority, and dominion? Seek the Lord for a deeper understanding and application of your unlimited power as you study these declarations.

1. I have the authority to walk on snakes and scorpions and overcome all the power of the enemy, and nothing will hurt me (Luke 10:19 GNT).
2. I have the power and authority to drive out all demons and to cure diseases (Luke 9:1 NIV).

Prophetic Prayer Declarations

3. I have the shield of salvation; God has enlarged my path so my feet will not slip. (Psalm 18:35-36 GNT).
4. I have every place where I set my foot (Joshua 1:3 NIV).
5. I am the head and not the tail; I am above only, and I will not be beneath (Deuteronomy 28:13 AMP).
6. I am calm as a baby when besieged. When all hell breaks loose, I'm collected and cool (Psalm 27:3 MSG).
7. I will not be tempted beyond what I can bear. But when I am tempted, God will provide a way out so that I can endure it (1 Corinthians 10:13 NIV).
8. I believe everything is possible with God. I can do all things through Christ, who strengthens and empowers me to fulfill His purpose. I am self-sufficient in Christ's sufficiency; I am ready for anything and equal to anything through Him, who infuses me with inner strength and confident peace (Mark 9:23 and Philippians 4:13).
9. I am strengthened with all power according to God's glorious might so that I may have great endurance and patience (Colossians 1:11).

Declarations for Power, Authority, and Dominion

10. I decree that every enemy who rises up against me will be defeated. They will come from one direction but flee from me in seven ways (Deuteronomy 28:7 NIV).
11. I declare that I shall flourish like a palm tree. I will have a long life and be upright and useful. I shall grow like a cedar in Lebanon. I shall flourish in the courts of our God. I shall bear fruit in old age. I shall be fresh and flourishing. The LORD is my Rock! (Psalm 92:12-15 NIV).
12. I shall decree a thing, and it shall be established. I will succeed in whatever I choose to do, and light will shine on the road ahead of me (Job 22:28 KJV, NLT).
13. I declare that I shall say to any mountain, 'Go, throw yourself into the sea,' without doubting, but believe that what I say will happen, it will be done for me (Mark 11:23).
14. I am made in God's image, after His likeness, to rule over the fish of the sea and the birds of the air, over the livestock, and over all the earth itself and every creature that crawls upon it. I have dominion over the fish of the sea and over the birds of the heavens and over every living thing that moves on the earth (Genesis 1: 26 BSB; 28b KJV).

Prophetic Prayer Declarations

15. When I walk through the Valley of Weeping, it will become a place of springs where pools of blessing and refreshment collect after the rains! I go from strength to strength. I grow constantly in strength (Psalms 84:6-7 TLB).
16. I am filled with the knowledge of God's will through all the wisdom and understanding that the Spirit of the LORD gives (Colossians 1:9).
17. I declare that as I send out the Word of God, people are healed and delivered from their destructions (Psalm 107:20 NKJV).
18. I am strengthened and spiritually energized with power through His Spirit in my inner self (Ephesians 3:16 AMP).
19. The mighty power at work in me is far above all rule and authority, power and dominion, and every name that is invoked, not only in the present age but also in the one to come (Ephesians 1:19-21).
20. God's plans are for me to prosper and to give me hope and a future (Jeremiah 29:11 NIV).
21. God is working in me, giving me the desire and the power to do what pleases him. I do everything without complaining and arguing so that I may become blameless and pure. I live clean, innocent lives as children of God, shining like

Declarations for Power, Authority, and Dominion

bright lights in a world full of crooked and perverse people (Philippians 2:13-15 NLT; 15a NIV).

Prophetic Prayer Declarations

Date _____

Reflection

1. What specific areas do you need to take authority over, and how? Write down your revelations.

_____

_____

_____

_____

_____

_____

_____

_____

_____

_____

_____

_____

Cast your burden on the Lord, and he will sustain you; he will never permit the righteous to be moved..
-Psalm 55:22 (ESV)

Declarations for Power, Authority, and Dominion

2. Reflect on declarations 14, 15, and 19. Write down your revelations.

_____
_____
_____
_____
_____
_____
_____
_____
_____
_____
_____
_____
_____
_____
_____
_____

I know all the things you do, and I have opened a door for you that no one can close.
-Revelations 3:8a (NLT)

Chapter 7
Declarations for Courage and Overcoming Fear

God has given believers a spirit not of fear but of power, love, and self-control. To succeed in every fearful situation, we must be strong and courageous, not frightened or dismayed, because the LORD is with us wherever we go. Despite David's stature, he defeated Goliath, a giant, with a sling and stones (1 Samuel 17). David approached Goliath with faith in God, confidence, and courage. You can face challenges with courage and unwavering faith to achieve an unconventional result. Is there anything dreadful troubling you? Ask the LORD to replace the spirit of timidity with courage as you study these declarations.

1. I am strong and very courageous! I am not afraid or discouraged. For the LORD my God is with me wherever I go (Joshua 1:9 NLT).

Declarations for Courage and Overcoming Fear

2. The LORD will never leave me nor forsake me." Deuteronomy 31:6b NIV For He will order his angels to protect me wherever I go" (Psalm 91:11-12 NLT).
3. I will not be afraid even when walking through the darkest valley, for God is close beside me, guarding and guiding me all the way (Psalm 23:4 TLB).
4. When I pass through deep waters, the LORD will be with me. And through the rivers, they shall not overflow me. When I walk through the fire, I shall not be burned, nor shall the flame scorch me (Isaiah 43:1-2 NKJV).
5. As I seek the LORD on the authority of His Word, He answers me. And delivers me from all my fears (Psalm 34:4 AMP).
6. I will not fear, though the earth do change, and the mountains be shaken. God is my refuge and strength, a very present help in times of trouble (Psalms 46: 2,1 ASV).
7. I give all my worries and cares to God, for He cares about me (1 Peter 5:7 NLT). I do not worry about tomorrow, for tomorrow will worry about itself (Matthew 6:34 NIV).
8. I do not worry about my life, what I will eat or drink, or about my body, what I will wear. Life is

more than food, and the body is more than clothes. My Heavenly Father knows that I need them. I seek first his kingdom and his righteousness, and all these things will be given to me as well (Matthew 6:25, 32-33 NIV).
9. I look to you, LORD, for help so I will be radiant with joy; no shadow of shame will darken my face (Psalm 34:5 NLT).
10. I am not afraid of the thousands of enemies who surround me on every side, for there are more on my side than on theirs (Psalm 3:6 GNT and 2 Kings 6:16 NLT).
11. I am not afraid. The LORD is with me! He is my God—nothing terrifies me! He has made me strong and will help me; He will protect and save me (Isaiah 41:10 GNT).
12. I am strengthened by the LORD. He protects me from the evil one (2 Thessalonians 3:3 NIV).
13. I cast all my cares, all my anxieties, all my worries, and all my concerns, once and for all on the LORD, for He cares about me with deepest affection and watches over me very carefully (1 Peter 5:6-7 AMP).
14. With God on my side, I'm fearless, afraid of no one and nothing. What can man do to me? (Psalms 27:1 MSG and Psalm 118:6b ESV).

Declarations for Courage and Overcoming Fear

15. I am not anxious or worried about anything, but in everything, every circumstance and situation, I continue to make my specific requests known to God through prayer and petition with thanksgiving (Philippians 4:6 AMP).
16. I have the Spirit of courage, not of fear but of power, love, and self-control (2 Timothy 1:6-7 ESV).
17. I am not afraid of those who kill the body but cannot kill the soul. Rather, I fear the One who can destroy both soul and body in hell (Matthew 10:28 NIV).
18. I commit everything I do to the LORD. I trust him, and He will help me (Psalm 37:5 NKJV).
19. I am confident that He who began a good work in me will carry it on to completion until the day of Christ Jesus (Philippians 1:6 NIV).
20. Through my faith in God, I have boldness and access to confidence. My faith gives me sufficient courage to approach God freely and openly through Christ (Ephesians 3:12).
21. I trust in the LORD with all my heart; I do not depend on my own understanding. I seek His will in all I do, and He will show me which path to take (Proverbs 3:5-6 NLT).

Prophetic Prayer Declarations

Date _____

Reflection

1. Which of the declarations in this chapter do you need to come alive in you the most and why? Write down your revelations.

_____

_____

_____

_____

_____

_____

_____

_____

_____

_____

_____

_____

For I am the Lord your God who takes hold of your right hand and says to you, Do not fear; I will help you.
-Isaiah 41:13 (NIV)

Declarations for Courage and Overcoming Fear

2. What fears have you decided to let go? Write down your revelations.

_____
_____
_____
_____
_____
_____
_____
_____
_____
_____
_____
_____
_____
_____

I sought the Lord, and he answered me; he delivered me from all my fears. Those who look to him are radiant; their faces are never covered with shame.
-Psalm 34:4-5 (NIV)

Chapter 8
Declarations for Victory in Spiritual Warfare

In spiritual warfare, believers must understand that we fight from a position of victory, not defeat. We combat the enemy through the good fight of faith until victory manifests. Shadrach, Meshach, and Abednego showed their faith in God by refusing to bow down to worship the golden idol decreed by the king (Daniel 3:10-26). Despite being thrown into a blazing furnace for defying the king, God saved them. Are you fully on guard with the whole armor of God to stand against every one of the devil's schemes? As you study the declarations below, ask the LORD to help you defeat the enemy.

1. I put on the full armor of God, so I am able to resist the enemy's attacks. I take up the shield of faith, with which I can extinguish all the flaming arrows of the evil one (Ephesians 6:13,16).

Declarations for Victory in Spiritual Warfare

2. I declare though a thousand fall at my side, though ten thousand are dying around me, these evils will not touch me. I will only observe with my eyes and see the punishment of the wicked (Psalm 91:7 NLT; 8 NIV).
3. I shall be anointed with fresh oil (Psalm 92:10b). The LORD prepares a table before me in the presence of my enemies. He anoints my head with oil; my cup overflows (Psalms 23:5 NIV).
4. I will advance against a troop with the LORD's help; with my God, I can scale a wall (Psalm 18:29).
5. I will triumph over my enemies. God holds my head and shoulders above all who try to pull me down (Psalms 27:6 GNT, MSG).
6. When evil people attack me and try to kill me, they will stumble and fall (Psalm 27:2 GNT).
7. LORD, contend with those who contend with me; fight against those who fight against me. (Psalm 35:1 NIV).
8. I win every fight against forces, authorities, and against rulers of darkness and powers in the spiritual world (Ephesians 6:12 CEV).
9. I am rescued from dead-end alleys and dark dungeons (Colossians 1:13 MSG).

Prophetic Prayer Declarations

10. I decree and declare that no weapon formed against me shall prosper, and every tongue which rises against me in judgment I condemn (Isaiah 54:17).
11. I am more than a conqueror, and I gained an overwhelming victory through Him, who loved me so much that He died for me (Romans 8:37 AMP).
12. I cast down arguments, imaginations, and every high thing that exalts itself against the knowledge of God, bringing every thought into captivity to the obedience of Christ (2 Corinthians 10:5 NKJV).
13. I declare the LORD is my Alpha and Omega, the First and the Last, the Beginning and the End (Revelation 22:13). I do not need to fight in battles. I stand firm, hold my position, and I will see the deliverance the LORD will give me (2 Chronicles 20:17).
14. I declare God is for me. Who can be against me? I receive all things. No one can bring any charge against me. It is God who justifies. Who, then, is the one who condemns? No one (Romans 8: 31-34 NIV).
15. I decree and declare that even if I pick up snakes with my hands and drink deadly poison, it will not

Declarations for Victory in Spiritual Warfare

hurt me at all. I will place my hands on sick people, and they will get well (Mark 16:18 NIV).

16. I defeat the enemy by the blood of the Lamb and by my testimony. I lay my life for God (Revelation 12:11).
17. Because of the LORD's great love, I am not consumed, for his compassions never fail. They are new every morning; great is your faithfulness. The LORD is my portion; therefore, I will wait for him. (Lamentations 3:22-24).
18. Because I trust in the LORD, I will find new strength. I will soar high on wings like eagles. I will run and not grow weary. I will walk and not faint (Isaiah 40:31 NLT).
19. LORD keep my lamp burning and turn my darkness into light (Psalm 18: 28).
20. My hands are trained for battle; my arms can bend a bow of bronze. I have the shield of victory, and my right hand sustains me. I am armed with strength for battle; the LORD has made my adversaries bow at my feet (Psalm 18:34-35, 39).
21. I am hidden from the conspiracy of the wicked, from that noisy crowd of evildoers (Psalm 64:1).

Prophetic Prayer Declarations

Date _____

Reflection

1. How do you tackle spiritual warfare? Write down your revelations.

_____
_____
_____
_____
_____
_____
_____
_____
_____
_____
_____

Even though I walk through the darkest valley, I will fear no evil, for you are with me; your rod and your staff they comfort me.
-Psalm 23:4 (NIV)

Declarations for Victory in Spiritual Warfare

2. What does declaration 1 look like in your life? Write down your revelations.

_____
_____
_____
_____
_____
_____
_____
_____
_____
_____
_____
_____
_____

Let us fix our eyes on Jesus, the author and perfecter of our faith, who for the joy set before Him endured the cross, scorning its shame, and sat down at the right hand of the throne of God.
-Hebrews 12:2 (BSB)

Chapter 9
Declarations for Leadership and Stewardship

Spiritual gifts are often not just for ourselves but also for equipping others. Serving others involves the ability to lead responsibly and steward resources diligently. Moses was a servant leader whom God trusted to guide the Israelites out of Egypt. He demonstrated wisdom and diligence in managing the resources that God provided during their time in the wilderness. He empowered others to become leaders and humbly accepted constructive feedback from God and people. How are you stewarding your resources and those entrusted to your care? As you reflect on the declarations below, ask the LORD to mold you into a diligent, wise, and faithful steward.

1. I declare that I am wise. I decree that I will shine like the brightness of the heavens and will lead

Declarations for Leadership and Stewardship

many to righteousness, like the stars forever and ever (Daniel 12:3 NIV).

2. I lead a quiet and peaceable life in all godliness and honesty. My life is good and acceptable in the sight of God our Savior (1 Timothy 2:2-3, KJV).

3. I declare that the LORD will teach me His way. He will lead me on a straight path. I will not be defeated by my enemies. I decree I will see the goodness of the LORD in the land of the living (Psalm 27: 11-12).

4. Show me the right path, O LORD; point out the road for me to follow. Lead me by your truth and teach me, for you are the God who saves me. All day long, I put my hope in you (Psalm 25 NLT).

5. I decree the LORD will bless and keep me. The LORD will make His face shine upon me and be gracious to me. The LORD will lift His countenance upon me and give me peace (Numbers 6:24-26 ESV).

6. I declare I will dwell in the house of the LORD all the days of my life, beholding the beauty of the LORD and meditating in His temple. In the day of trouble, I declare the LORD will conceal me in His tabernacle. In the secret place of His tent, the LORD will hide me. He will lift me up on a rock. I

Prophetic Prayer Declarations

declare my head will be lifted above my enemies around me (Psalm 27: 4-6 NASB).

7. I declare the LORD will give me the key to authority in His house. Whenever I open any door, no enemy will be able to close it. When I close doors, no enemy will be able to open them. I will bring honor to my family name, for the LORD will drive me firmly in place like a nail in the wall. I will bring honor to even the lowest members of my family (Isaiah 22: 22-24 NIV).
8. I declare I shall be strong and do exploits (Daniel 11:32 KJV).
9. I decree that my gifts will make room for me and bring me before great men (Proverbs 18:16 NKJV).
10. I declare the favor of the LORD our God is upon me. He will establish the work of my hands (Psalm 90:17 ESV).
11. I declare the LORD shines on me, and people will see His glory on me. Nations will come to my light; kings will come to the brightness of my sunrise (Isaiah 60:2-3).
12. I declare God has anointed me with the oil of gladness more than my companions (Psalms 45:7 NJKV).

Declarations for Leadership and Stewardship

13. I do nothing out of selfish ambition or vain conceit. Rather, in humility, I value others above myself, not looking to my own interests but to the interests of others (Philippians 2:3-4 NIV).
14. I obey my leaders and submit to them. I do this joyfully, not groaning (Hebrews 13:17 ESV).
15. I am a servant of Christ and steward of the mysteries of God. I declare I will be found trustworthy (1 Corinthians 4:1-2 NASB).
16. I declare that I will not labor in vain. The LORD will build my house and watch over my city (Psalm 127:1).
17. I pray in the Spirit at all times and on every occasion. I stay alert and persistent in my prayers for all believers everywhere (Ephesians 6:18 NLT)
18. I walk in a manner worthy of the calling to which I have been called, with all humility and gentleness, with patience, bearing with one another in love, eager to maintain the unity of the Spirit in the bond of peace (Ephesians 4:1-3 ESV).
19. I recognize the LORD when He speaks in my dreams, in visions, and whispers in my ears (Job 33:14-16).

Prophetic Prayer Declarations

20. I shall seek the LORD and find Him when I search for Him with all my heart (Jeremiah 29:13 KJV).
21. As for me and my household, we will serve the LORD (Joshua 24:15b NIV).

Declarations for Leadership and Stewardship

Date _____

Reflection

1. In what ways or areas has the LORD prompted you to lead? Write down your revelations.

_____
_____
_____
_____
_____
_____
_____
_____
_____
_____
_____
_____

Be an example to all believers in what you say, in the way you live, in your love, your faith, and your purity.
- 1 Timothy 4:12b (NLT)

Prophetic Prayer Declarations

2. Reflect on declaration 14. What have you been tasked to steward? Write down your revelations.

_____
_____
_____
_____
_____
_____
_____
_____
_____
_____
_____
_____
_____
_____
_____
_____

For the Lord gives wisdom; from his mouth come knowledge and understanding.
- Proverbs 2:6 (ESV)

Chapter 10
Declarations for Restoration

Restoration is the act of returning something to its original state. When Satan attacked Job and he lost everything he owned, he never cursed God. Instead, he held on to his faith even in the face of adversity until God restored his fortunes, giving him twice what he had before. Where are you seeking restitution or revival? Seek the LORD's face to regain all that you have lost as you study these declarations.

1. I am forgetting what happened and have stopped going over old history. I am alert and present. God is about to do something brand-new in my life. It's bursting out! I see it. There it is! God is making a road through the desert and giving me streams of water there (Isaiah 43:18-19 MSG).
2. I will surely forget any misery I have experienced. It will be like water flowing away. I decree my life

will be brighter than the noonday. Even darkness will be as bright as morning (Job 11:16-17 NLT).
3. I decree the LORD is making all things new. I receive a new heart and a new spirit within me (Revelation 21:5 and Ezekiel 36:26).
4. I am restored from the depths of the earth. I will increase in honor and comfort once more (Psalm 71:20-21).
5. LORD, restore the years that the enemy has consumed. I shall eat in plenty and be satisfied. I shall praise the name of the LORD my God, Who has worked wonders for me. I shall never be put to shame (Joel 2:25-26 NKJV).
6. LORD, restore the joy of Your salvation and grant me a willing spirit to sustain me. (Psalm 51:12 NIV).
7. I shall have double honor instead of shame. I shall rejoice in double portion instead of confusion. I shall possess a double portion in this land, and everlasting joy shall be mine (Isaiah 61:7 NKJV).
8. I receive a crown of beauty instead of ashes, the oil of joy instead of mourning, and a garment of praise instead of a spirit of despair. I will be called oaks of righteousness, a planting of the LORD to display his splendor (Isaiah 61:3 NIV).

Declarations for Restoration

9. I receive renewed strength from the LORD. I am guided along the path of righteousness, bringing honor to the LORD's name (Psalms 23:3).
10. LORD, restore my health and heal all my wounds. I receive health and healing. And I will enjoy abundant peace and security (Jeremiah 30:17; 33:6).
11. Heal me, LORD, and I will be healed; save me, and I will be saved, for you are the one I praise (Jeremiah 17:14).
12. I am healed from a broken heart and wounds. The LORD heals my pain and comforts my sorrow (Psalm 147:3 AMP).
13. I pray that I enjoy good health and that all goes well with me, even as my soul prospers (3 John 1:2).
14. I am called by God's name. I humble myself, pray, and seek the LORD's face. As I turn away from wicked ways, the LORD will hear me, forgive my sins, and heal me (2 Chronicles 7:14 NIV).
15. I declare the LORD will make me renowned and praised among all the peoples of the earth and restore my fortunes before my eyes (Zephaniah 3:20).

Prophetic Prayer Declarations

16. I shall restore the foundations of many generations. I shall be called the repairer of broken walls, the restorer of homes (Isaiah 58:12).
17. I have the Spirit of the LORD in me. He has anointed me to proclaim good news to the poor. He has sent me to proclaim liberty to the captives and recovering of sight to the blind, to set at liberty those who are oppressed (Luke 4:18 ESV).
18. I shall rebuild the ruined cities and inhabit them; I shall plant vineyards and drink their wine, and I shall make gardens and eat their fruit (Amos 9:14 ESV).
19. I lift up my eyes to the hills. From where does my help come? My help comes from the LORD, who made heaven and earth. He will not let my foot be moved; he who keeps me will not slumber. Behold, he who keeps Israel will neither slumber nor sleep. The LORD is my keeper and my shade on my right hand (Psalm 121:1-8 ESV).
20. I cast my cares on the LORD, and He will sustain me. He will never let me be shaken (Psalm 55:22).
21. I am restored, confirmed, strengthened, and established by God (1 Peter 5:10).

Declarations for Restoration

Date _____

Reflection

1. What comes to mind as you reflect on declaration 5? What do you want restored? Write down your revelations.

_____

_____

_____

_____

_____

_____

_____

_____

_____

_____

_____

Restore to me the joy of Your salvation,
And uphold me by Your generous Spirit.
-Psalm 51:12 (NKJV)

Prophetic Prayer Declarations

2. Which of the restoration declarations do you want to meditate on, this season and why? Write down your revelations.

_____

_____

_____

_____

_____

_____

_____

_____

_____

_____

_____

_____

_____

_____

_____

After Job had prayed for his friends, the Lord restored his fortunes and gave him twice as much as he had before.
-Job 42:10 (NIV)

Note to Reader

Dear Reader,

Thank you for reading my book. I hope its content has blessed you.

As a new author, I would greatly appreciate it if you could share how God blessed or helped you through this book by emailing Kemi@DrKemiAkintewe.com or leaving a review on Amazon so that others may benefit from your experience.

I love engaging with my readers about any of my books, so feel free to connect with me on social media or via email.

Also, please let me know if you would like to be notified about new releases, courses, workshops, conferences, or my coaching programs. If you are looking for a speaker or facilitator for your faith-based events, don't hesitate to reach out for my availability.

Thank you for the opportunity to serve you in this capacity.

Blessings,

Kemi Akintewe

Dr. Kemi Akintewe

Educator |Success Coach |Author

Kemi@DrKemiAkintewe.com

About the Author

Dr. Kemi Akintewe is a warrior for Christ and a laborer in His vineyard. She leads a Prophetic, Prayer, and Deliverance ministry in Tampa, Florida. She is passionate about helping believers activate the gift of prophecy and coaching others to discover and launch their spiritual gifts.

Originally born in Washington, D.C., and raised in Nigeria, West Africa, Dr. Akintewe is an engineering professor, a military wife, and the mother of two children. She is an inspirational, professional, certified success coach and a conscientious mentor who believes everyone can reach their full potential by positioning themselves for God to do His work. She is also the author of the following books:

- **Goal Redeemer:** 10 Principles for Overcoming Barriers to Achieving Your Goals and Fulfilling Your God-Given Dreams
- **Goal Redeemer Planner Journal** -Creating the Life I Desire
- **Prophetic Activations Workbook:** A 10-Week Practical Exercise for Launching Your Prophetic Gift

Dr. Akintewe conducts faith-based empowerment sessions and goal-setting workshops at various local and international institutions.

Contact Information:
Kemi@DrKemiAkintewe.com
www.DrKemiAkintewe.com

www.ingramcontent.com/pod-product-compliance
Lightning Source LLC
Chambersburg PA
CBHW060337050426
42449CB00011B/2779